BITTERSWEET

DL FOWLER

Without limiting the rights under the copyright reserved below, no part of this publication may be reproduced, stored in or introduced into a retrieval system, or transmitted, in any form or by any means (electronic, mechanical, photocopying, recording, or otherwise) without prior written permission of the copyright holder.

Copyright © DL Fowler 2018.
All rights reserved.

For additional information
Visit http://dlfowler.com

ISBN: 978-0-9963805-2-2

Published in the United States.
Harbor Hill Publishing.

CONTENTS

Hope 11
- Endless Dreams 13
- Fork in the Road 14
- My-opia 15
- Nature Walk 16
- Indian Paintbrush 18

Danger 19
- Perspective 21
- Simplicity 23
- Sequestered 24
- Strange Things 26
- Different Not Deficient 27
- Pleasantville 29
- Dark 30
- Light's Beauty 31

Lost 33
- Layers of Me 35
- Soul Searching 37
- A Place 38
- Passage 40
- #metoo 42
- Without Arms 44
- Two lives 45
- Gardening 46
- Waking to Royalty 49
- Gentle 51

Fallen 53
- Siren's Call 55
- Peace 57
- Patriots 59
- Supremacy 61
- God's Whore Whines 62
- God's Whore 64

Wisdom	66
My Heart Bleeds	67
Whispers	69
Shadows	70

Elements 75

Wind	77
Rain	78
Fire	79
Stars	80

Essays 81

Indigo	83
Healing	85
Tyrone	87
Earth	89

Poems & Essays

Inspiration

From the depths of our unconscious,
A hand we cannot shackle
Claws at our heart,
And in our desperation,
Against our stiff rebellion,
Comes unrelenting truth
By the bittersweet grace of God.

Adapted from the Oresteia by Aeschylus (ca 460 BC)

HOPE

ENDLESS DREAMS

Some dreams fade in morning light,
Others, implode in thunderous night,
Drenched in sweat and steeped in fright.
There are dreamless spells
Full of empty wells,
When hope thirsts, but nothing quells.
Dreams can die, though not alone,
But chained 'round necks, like heavy stones,
To drowning dreamers with dying groans.

Dream the dream that never ends
Of a place where known with unknown blends,
Pursue the path each tireless dreamer wends
Until the world, along that arc, tumultuously bends.

FORK IN THE ROAD

Right or left, either way,
Take it!
You'll get there just the same
Passing trees on either side,
If not trees, cactus then
With tumbleweed blown
Across your path,
Or rocks, ravines, placid lakes,
Glaciers hanging from mountain crags,
Raging rivers, ocean beaches,
Rows of corn or soybean,
Whichever way you go
Take a trail to some place new.
Don't worry if it isn't safe,
Or maybe it'll be worse
Than where you are.
Just move along,
Nothing ever ends,
There are only new beginnings.

MY-OPIA

My editor suggested someone should write a happy poem, so here goes:

If only we weren't so my-opic
If we could crawl under the other guy's skin
Not in a negative way, I mean,
And see the world through his eyes
Touch the soil with someone else's feet
Bleed that other gal's blood
We could shake our addiction to my-opia
And the world would be happier place.
If only we weren't so my-opic ...
Oh well ...

NATURE WALK

Absorbed, I was by fruitless searches
For riches and lofty perches,
While blanched images stole my thoughts,
Displacing dreams with weighty oughts,
Fixing my mind on work and duty,
Though surrounded by graceful beauty,
Until one day, on a hillside resting,
I quit all voracious questing.
About the time for evening vesper
I heard a birch tree whisper,
Safe from ears of lurking thieves,
"There's gold here in my seasoned leaves."

Now possessing new insight,
Illumined by angelic light,
Reprieved from toil's demand,
I feast upon prior contraband
Embracing less burdensome life
Gaining joy midst labor's strife
Seeing things that always were,
But never gave me stir.

Clutching the hem of autumn's charm
A frosty spectre provokes alarm
For all except a maple tree,
Resisting what's meant to be.
In crimson regimental dress,

Undaunted by death's certain press,
It's cloak more brilliant as nights draw cool
It accepts the challenge of winter's duel.

Folded in deep secluded woods,
Martyred by late winter floods,
Littered with much debris,
A stifled stream seeks the sea,
Not confined to rigid course
But, guided by a mystic force.
With a weaver's artistry,
It carves a complex tapestry
Calmly through the forest floor,
Winding toward a distant shore,
Nurturing the web of life—
Nature's mother, but no one's wife.

An undistinguished springtime bird,
Which leaves men's hearts unstirred,
Joins eagles at stream-side play,
But is promptly chased away.
Grace, nonetheless, buoys its flight,
While nature fails to see its blight,
And given another year,
The aberrant bird will be their peer.

All these things I now see clear
As beauty transcends life's harried blur.
Even the oak in sunset inspired lace
Edging its ruby, radiant face,
Draws my enchanted stare
As autumn returns with its sweet-scented air.

INDIAN PAINTBRUSH

Found lacing rocky trailsides
And adorning alpine meadows
In hues of silver, jade, and orange,
Stalks of Castilleja mimic
A host of artists' brushes
Painting opuses of inner worlds
On canvases fresh and blank,
Inspired by myriad tribulations,
Yet with a single palette shared.

DANGER

PERSPECTIVE

The raptor swoops,
A rodent cowers,
Assimilated in the grasses.
If it lives 'til daylight passes
A trillion stars may emerge,
Any pair of which could be
The deadly glare
Of a waiting,
Hungry owl.
A million, million raptors
And likewise stealthy owls
Scan daily for ill-fated prey,
While many more of varmints
Seek refuge from their claws.

Beneath a ceiling of golden tiles,
At a table set with silver,
A Diospyros throne, jeweled,
Studded with ill-gotten ivories,
Bears an oligarchy prince,
Ravishing chateaubriand for one.
All the while, unnoticed,
A master's priceless homage
Hangs upon the wall behind—
Apostles, twelve, and humble Christ
Partaking bread and wine.
Nearby, in a hostile alley,

A threadbare child
Nibbles moldy crust
Scavenged from a refuse bin;
Its dearth of scraps
Bears testimony to
The oligarch's greed.

Vanity, vanity,
All is in vain.
Where can hope be found?

Beyond myriad galaxies,
Which charm the midnight sky,
Lives a sun that never dies,
In whose orbit
All universes turn,
Where time unwinds,
Erasing polluted pasts,
Where justice mourns no more,
Where wounds and death can't sting,
Where prey share raptors' nests,
And urchins with oligarchs dance.

SIMPLICITY

Simplicity
Is a subtle con
Like racing to
A dim-lit corner
At the sound of
Footsteps in the dark.
How's the lamppost going to help?
Simplicity
Substitutes for truth
When the latter is inconvenient,
Worse yet, when it requires work.

SEQUESTERED

I. Lamented Sequestration

> The rapier of desertion,
> Thrust by deceit and betrayal,
> Like a matador's blade
> Slices flesh,
> Glances off bone,
> Splaying open old wounds.
> An honest friend
> Would be welcomed,
> But none comes.

II. Inescapable Sequestration

> No common ground,
> No celebrated vanguard
> Who, in going before,
> Gleaned wisdom
> From this lofty perch
> To pass along.
> Even a legend,
> Though being unreal,
> Would be a kindred soul.

III. Welcome Sequestration

> Fire feasts on sooted,
> Corroding cedar,
> Sparks of amber, rust, and red

Ascend and fall.
Stacks of logs
Await their turn
To dissipate in time.
Snowflakes on a window
Flutter downward,
Teased by icy wind,
Leaving in their wakes
Silent trails of tears.
On distant vales,
Undisturbed by man or beast,
Shiny crystals kiss carpets
Laid by prior fallen snows.

STRANGE THINGS

In perceptible space,
Seams, as though
Re-signed portals,
Lure us from
The plain upside
We're mired in,
To other mirrored
Parfaitic lairs below, with
Alien sights and sounds,
Presumed distortions,
Nonetheless, truly parfaitic,
Until swirled into a hole
As if whole.
A stranger thing,
Not only up and down,
If one other, why not more?
Why not up and down and over,
Over and over again?
Strangest thing,
Binary choices, such as one or lost.

DIFFERENT NOT DEFICIENT

Some things are dark while others are light
Take the difference between black and white.
Mountains are high and valleys lie low
Leaves in autumn turn scarlet or yellow
Lakes languish, but rivers flow
Water is sometimes rain or snow
Knots may square or curl in a bow
Old fires smolder, yet new flames glow
Some birds chirp when others crow
Geese lay eggs and fish plant roe
This list may never end, you know
I can make it stop or grow,
Now let's add Hank and Moe
Or Mary and Jo
How about Smith and Enloe?
Any unbalanced row
We could just throw
The lesser of each could go.

One and three, or two and four
Contrary rhythms tapped on a floor,
Must one stop for the other to soar?
So, which is lesser and which is more?
Why pick just one to adore,
When surprises lurk in every score,
And difference does not make one poor?
Cross-beats played across the shore

Reflect life's polyrhythmic core,
Its contradictory nature
Gives universal nurture.
Why settle for a zero sum game
When diversity is a beautiful name?
A whole is greater than its summed parts,
Normal is not the object of arts.

PLEASANTVILLE

Pleasantville puts on a tranquil face,
Shrubs trimmed,
Lush, green lawns,
Neighbors smiling in peace,
Serenity masking fissures.
Beneath its clean, swept streets
In catacombs imprisoned,
Hordes of grisly ghouls—
Right, left, right steppers,
Polyrhythmic drummers,
Maestros versed in
Harmonic contradictions—
Plot to strip off
Pleasantville's façade,
And expose its oppression of
God-given genius.

DARK

I don't look for it,
It comes for me,
Then turns off the light.
Dark is parasitic, living in my eyes.
When eyes go dark, it takes my breath.
After breath, it eats the heart.
Folks who never suffer dark,
Haven't got a clue
Of how to hold things tight
When dark sucks out the glue.
Only two things conquer dark,
Death or light.
So, if you cannot find a switch,
There's only one choice left.
Or, maybe you can grab a candle,
And happen to have a match,
So if you keep the damn thing lit,
You'll find your way back home.

LIGHT'S BEAUTY

Cowering by a roadside,
In paralytic stupor,
Despair falls prey to fear,
Watching night consume night,
Black envelope black,
Dark devour dark.
Dark flaunts its gluttony,
Esteems the vain,
Crushes the meek,
Shames the naked,
Robs the poor,
Emboldens liars,
Martyrs saints,
Starves orphans,
Shackles slaves,
Rapes our mothers, sisters, daughters.
Dark erodes hope, but hope doesn't die.
When beacons pierce the fog,
Or headlights round the bend,
When lightning flashes in a storm,
Or the moon slips between clouds,
When stars mark the northern sky,
Or dawn subdues night—
In those moments
Dark's reign ebbs,
Eclipsed by resilient hope.

LOST

LAYERS OF ME

Good god, no wonder
I can't be mastered—
You can't know me
By projecting yourself
Onto the many canvases
Of me.
Probe.
Peel back my layers.
Tread lightly on ancient
Wounds that never healed,
Festering in dank,
Un-illumined creases.
Heed
Commands of wary
Pockmarked demons
Snarling as you pass.
Fear
Gargoyles perched atop
Tall, thick walls
Built to test your resolve.
Did you bring something
To scale those walls,
Outflank them,
Penetrate them?
Foolishness!
The first rule of war—
Know your enemy

Strengths and weakness, both.
But why resort to war?
Maybe I want to be known,
Celebrated for who I am
By someone willing
To pay the price
Which the core of me demands.

SOUL SEARCHING

A cavern coils within my core,
Curving like a golden spiral,
With its portal unseen
By eyes trained on my veneer.
Many laud my gentle graces,
Delighting in my artistry,
Viewing what they want to see,
Just not the real me.
Deep within my secret enclave,
In a fortress dark, carved from stone,
Light flickers through a fissure,
A beacon only some can see,
Not a beckon to be rescued,
But an invitation to approach,
To discover my deepest essence,
To touch my very soul.

A PLACE

There's a place we're born into
Where we don't want to stay
And in the hell we wander through
We find it hard to pray.

My father chased myriad schemes
He couldn't quite fulfill
He sometimes tried to curb my dreams
By disparaging my will.

My mother was a shadow's blur
The darkness made her wilt.
But when I tried to rescue her
She filled me with her guilt.

In my dreams I dared to try
To sail the wide blue sea,
But woke certain I was haunted by
My father's ghost in me.

Some things only I can see
And only I can choose
But deep within the core of me
I fear I'm born to lose.

My only hope is standing tall
Like a giant redwood tree

And reaching to the sky for all
That I am meant to be.

There is a place we struggle through
Where we don't want to stay,
But if we steer our own true course
We're bound to find our way.

PASSAGE

I came upon a passage
A narrow slit at best
Not only skinny;
But squat, as well.
I wondered how
One passes through
When encumbered
By a bulky load.

I shed my baggage,
Arranging it in orderly stacks,
And averse to waste and litter,
I could not leave a single piece behind.
Imagine if I did, and
Following my example,
Others did the same,
What a mess we'd make.
Each piece I tried
One by one
To angle through
To the other side.
All to no avail.
Beads of sweat,
Aching limbs, and
Calloused hands
Summed to my reward.
For what purpose, though?

I'd spent a lifetime
Gathering stuff,
Now going forward
None of it fit,
Which raises a question—
If my stuff isn't wanted,
How wanted am I?
I stare at the tiny portal
And ask myself,
If that's the case,
Do I really want to go?

#METOO

At first it seeps,
Next, it trickles,
Still contained and private,
But as the memory grows
It laps the shoreline of my mind,
Teasing out misplaced guilt
And unrelenting ghosts—
Boxing gloves meant for manning up
Though barely out of diapers,
Matched against a bully
Who doesn't know when to quit.
Bed-wetting follows.
Memories lost of tender years.

Then after my childhood fog
A man invades my space,
Catching me by surprise.
A big time Boy Scout,
Valued and esteemed,
The kind who hugs
While saying thanks,
So he can grab your ass
And squeeze it hard.
But in the aftershock
Even though I did no wrong,
There's no place safe to crawl into,
No one I can tell.

You sure it happened
The way you say?
He's done so much, for many ...
What's your angle, anyway?
Fifteen seconds of fame?
For him,
It was just a flash in time,
And maybe you see it that way, too.
But for me ...
Greying whiskers,
Abrasive against my face,
Lingering doubts of
Where I went wrong,
All these remain—
A fifty-year wound.

WITHOUT ARMS

Smoke and fire belch
From windows, doors, roofs, cars
Sirens whine, stabbing the night,
A black canvass stained
With orange and red bursts
Silhouetted by steel-blue,
Greyish ghosts.
Mobbing hordes in a
Rope-less tug-of-war
With agents of oppressors
Whose only need is greed.
Bodies all around,
Some bellow angry shouts
Others vomit groans.
Someone yells, "Run,
Stop for nothing, no one."
Their words swirl
In an endless loop
Just outside my reach.
My feet are anchored,
Swallowed by sorrow,
Not abducted by fear,
But frozen in the memory
Of children drawing pictures
Of people with no arms
Moments before Dr. King was shot.

TWO LIVES

He was before I was me.
I wasn't there, but I was there in him.
He's gone now, but still is here in me.
If not him, his nightmares, then
Coursing terror through my veins —
Live ammo whizzing past his head,
Whistles in my ears,
The rata-tat-tat of firing pins,
Playing a backbeat for his sprint,
Rattles my teeth,
Quaking limbs and burning lungs
While racing to a spot once regarded safe,
A bleeding friend slung over his back,
His fatigue drains my strength.

I wasn't there, but I was there in him,
My nightmares joining his,
His wounds compounding mine.
Who knows how many lives
Are borne in me
Or how many lives I've lived,
Though never having died,
All melding into one,
As if one life's worth of wounds
Isn't pain enough?

GARDENING

I started a garden in my youth,
Rows carefully planned
Colors subdued, shrubs trim
A tribute to balance and control
An opus of order it appeared to be
But it wasn't the real me.

I strolled my garden path one day
As I had always done
But as I reached the usual bend
My feet just wouldn't turn.
So, straight I set my rebel course,
With no particular place in mind,
Wading through vines and thorns.

Along this unplanned journey
I found a gurgling brook
Which seemed to bid me
'Stop for a while,'
A call I could not resist.
So sitting beside this talking stream
My gaze began to drift
And I spotted another trail,
Which my feet agreed to follow
Until somewhere in the wild
I stood at the edge of a cliff.

I sat upon the very brink
Of this windblown precipice
Where instantly my hands began
A flower to caress.
This flower was a different kind
From those I tended before
Brilliant, sturdy
No furrowed rows
No stone-lined paths
Freedom, or so it seemed.

Returning to my garden
Doing my normal chores,
I listened for that flower's voice
And rushed off when it called,
Flying into its open arms
Losing myself in dance, and
Somewhere in its siren song
Before I left its side,
My flower let me touch its soul
Making me yearn for more,
But duty bound, my garden
I could not ignore.

Days passed into night times
Silent, lonely, and bleak,
No flower calling my name.
So to that precipice I returned,
Which had once given me joy,
And found a limp, barren stalk
That filled my heart with grief.
The flower no longer lived.

It had lost its hope in me.

As I passed my days
On the edge of life,
Yearning for what I had lost
My garden sat in disarray,
Overgrown with weeds,
Color gone, shrubs turned brown,
A picture of neglect.
Then one dawn, by Nature's clock
In the gnarled scrub of that poor plot,
Seeds appeared of every sort,
Many I had long forgotten,
Each which sprouted into a plant
More remarkable than my youthful plan,
Making my garden my dream.

WAKING TO ROYALTY

I awoke one day
Peering at the portrait of
Of a Queen,
But plainly dressed
With her face stained
By the residue of toil.
For some reason,
Only I could see
Her royalty.
She seemed out of place,
The owner lacking awareness
Of the value this jewel might bring
To one such as me,
Nor the awe in which Majesty
Rightly, should be held.
I offered to buy the piece,
But it was not for sale.
So, I tried to paint her face anew,
As it always should have been.
With careful strokes,
I laid each strand of hair.
With bold lines,
I captured the strength of her chin.
With elegant arches,
I defined the grace of her neck.
With laced bodices,
I bounded the sanctuary of her bosom.

When the canvas would not
Translate my imagination,
I tried to sculpt her from supple clay.
I held her cheeks gently in my hands.
I traced the beacon of her neck.
Her throat trembled at my touch.
My hands drank in her power
As they ventured along
The edges of her shoulders, and
Over her sweet breasts
To a holy spot, where in awe
Life resounded through her soul.
But this masterpiece
Still was not my Queen.
In truth, we cannot own royalty.
We must find the Queen within ourselves.

GENTLE

Gentle souls live here too,
The world's their home,
As well as yours, so
Why are they required to die
In order to survive?
They must steel their hearts,
Build walls of stone,
Pump molten lava through their veins,
Spew vitriol from their mouths,
Gather where they haven't sown,
Harvest what they did not till
Hoard crops they didn't reap,
Eat bread earned
By another's sweat,
Scramble over weaker backs,
Calculate their gains and losses,
Despise what they have become—
Monsters just like you—
Hiding their shame behind iron masks,
Stifling every urge to grieve
Lest the eyeholes rust from salty tears.
Why can't you just let gentle be?

FALLEN

SIREN'S CALL

It's often told that long ago
As ancient mariners traversed the sea,
Sailing past enchanted isles,
Sirens beckoned, "Come"
Luring them off their course.
Once ashore, transfixed,
Imprisoned by the enchantress' spell,
Forgetful of their recent freedom,
Willful servants they'd become.

For that reason I've avoided
Travel on uncharted oceans
Chafing as I've walked upon
Well-worn paths, others trod before.
It would be a great misstatement
Though, If I did not confess
I love to stand on rocky vistas
Absorbing there the steel-blue vastness
Of rolling, surging waves.

One day, descending to the water
Winding through a cypress grove
Of branches gnarled in knots,
I heard a voice droning faintly,
Drawing me with a plaintive call,
"Please, someone rescue me."
Desperation overwhelmed me

Like a monsoon flood,
As if I, myself, were drowning,
Helpless in the sea.

I raced up to the water's edge,
Not stopping, even to take a breath,
And braving the encroaching tide
I vaulted forth, churning, splashing
Until I could run no more.
Then scanning across the wide horizon,
Hoping to find a soul in need,
I found myself in peril's grip
As fleeting sand beneath my feet
Eroded by the pounding surf,
Opened up a gaping throat and
Swallowed me into its depths.

PEACE

Satin veiled cobalt waters,
Giving an illusion of peace
While in the depths below
Its currents roil and heave.

Gunmetal cannon poised over quiet détente
Two sides saying they're right.
Missiles don't fly, but words still wound,
And a tripwire lies in their path.

Voices silent at holiday meals,
Or muted as die Stechschritte echo past.
Arguing wanes, but oppression rises,
Leaving despots all the bolder.

Rhythmic waves massage a sandy cove,
Wildflowers bow in gentle breezes,
Snowflakes kiss without a sound,
Cotton candy clouds tinted by the setting sun,
Diamonds stretch across black desert nights,
Soft breathing of lovers sleeping,
Their differences forgotten for a little while—
All are illusions of peace.

True peace comes when no one's watching,
For a price we do not pay.
Peace falls like dew in the night

Spreading its mercy blindly
No exemptions, no exclusions
All are blessed the same—
Each blessed, though undeserving.

Contentment is the portico of peace
Forgiveness is its threshold
Equality its vestibule
Grace the great hallway
Communion is its table.
Acceptance is a feast, with
Love as its wine.
It's time we knew true peace.

PATRIOTS

One stands erect
At the foot of Old Glory
Another takes a knee.
Tales of ancient heroic feats,
No matter how well sanitized,
Make some chests swell
While others see a sea of sins.
The price of envied wealth—
Coffins from battlefields
At home and on distant shores—
Testifies to passions we clutch,
Fables, dreams, and principles
Upon which patriots do not agree.
Some see black and white,
Others glimpse varied hues,
While the trigger that
Should turn all eyes red
Is the Nazi and the KKK,
Who would sell their fellow man,
Tear children from mothers' breasts,
Wring sweat from another's brow,
Force-march millions from their homes
To feed their own pomposity,
Fuelling their lust for wealth and power
While tossing carcasses into open pits
To bulldoze over them with Mother Earth,

Traitors standing now in hallowed halls
Where ancient patriots,
Imperfect in their walk,
Though visionaries in their dreams,
Once trod.

SUPREMACY

Give me liberty
So, give me death.
Your death, rose.
Die rose die
You're in my seat
Die rose die
You breathe my air
Die rose die
You need my help
Die rose die
You're not my kind
Die rose die
Your blood and soil are mine
Die rose
Die for me.
For me.
Me, me, me.
Give me your liberty, rose.
Give me your life.
So I can have mine.
Just call me supreme.

GOD'S WHORE WHINES

If god wasn't so lazy,
Or maybe, just inept,
I'd never have to exploit,
There would be no point
To hording wealth,
No need to feed the hungry,
Give drink to the thirsty,
Host strangers,
Visit the imprisoned,
Protect widows,
Nurture a child,
Bring healing to the sick or
Clothing the naked,
There would be no least of these.

If god would, at least pretend,
To be sovereign of all the earth
I wouldn't usurp his power,
I wouldn't make laws
For controlling others,
I wouldn't wage war
Against infidels,
I'd patiently wait
For his plan to unfold
Instead of chasing
People from their land
To impose his kingdom

By force, plunder, or disease.

If god would just do his job,
We wouldn't need morality police,
We wouldn't need to punish sins,
I wouldn't wind up
Profaning his name
Or forgetting who he is.
I could trust in his grace and live.

Please, god, get off the dime
So I can be holy like you.

GOD'S WHORE

If god married a whore
Who crossed an ocean
To inflame a war,
Ending the peace he paid dearly for,
What would such a god do?

If she flaunted his love
While treating her neighbor
With spite and contempt,
What would such a god do?

If she begged for trifles
When he promised, unasked,
To meet all her needs
What would such a god do?

If she invoked his name
For selfish gain
Oh how vain!
What would such a god do?

If she gave to the rich
What belonged to the poor
To tighten her grip on power,
What would such a god do?

If she clamored for justice

But corrupted the law
And judged with lop-sided scales,
What would such a god do?

If she prized only the first
And last hours of life,
But pillaged the days in between,
What would such a god do?

If she drew on his power,
Making bread out of stones
Then bragged she'd done it all on her own,
What would such a god do?

If she leapt from a tower
With reckless abandon,
To prove salvation was due her,
What would such s god do?

If she dropped to her knees
Before princes and kings
Who promised her fame and glory,
What would such a god do?

If she twisted his truth
To cover her lies while
Turning his world against him,
What would such a god do
To prove the mystery of his love?

WISDOM

Seated at the feet of scholars
Sopping their collective genius,
We never grow any wiser
Than when we first began.
Reading every treatise penned
By leagues of erudite men,
Fails to give us answers
We hope to find therein.
Scorning dull, prosaic criers,
We turn to rash, seductive liars
Peddling fabricated knowledge
And muting curiosity's voice.

While we burrow under
Blankets of myth in our
Subterranean tombs of belief,
Deafened to reason and truth,
Reality is on the prowl—
Its honed, slashing claw
Poised to instruct.
No mercy will it allow.
The more ignorance we show,
The heavier its didactic blows,
Until our vanity is sapped,
And tumultuously we learn,
Else truth, long abandoned,
Becomes pointless by our death.

MY HEART BLEEDS

Passing through a crowded room,
Walking down a busy street,
Or perched on a distant vantage,
Others' pain stabs me uninvited
Without my knowing their names.
Mine are not common wounds
Healed by time and reason.
Only justice cures my grief
For so many hearts broken.

Those who carve these wounds of mine,
Wounds that ooze with others' blood,
Say my feelings run too deep,
My heart is far too tender.
I do not bleed by choice, though.
Even when victims do not speak,
Their silence pierces my soul,
And your deeds don't pass unnoticed.

Welts from wrath
That fuels their fear,
Bruises from brawn
That holds them down,
Injustice that keeps them in their place,
Again, again and once more.
You steal their innocence,
Rob them of joy,

Gorge on their tenderized flesh—
Or enable those who do.
Lather, rinse, repeat.

Remember you've been warned,
And this should make you shudder:
When you wound another,
My heart bleeds with God's,
And our blood is on your hands.

WHISPERS

A silhouetted figure, cast in amber light,
Disrobes unaware, in view of prying eyes.
Rapt by her beauty, he creeps ever nearer,
Up to her window, watching uninvited.
Shapely curves with honeyed skin
Arouse his libido, while
Firm breasts with nippled peaks
Prime his tongue for tasting.
Where's the harm in this?
Long after he finishes
Her soul laments in silent wails
Of shame, guilt, unfathomable loss—
The booty of his thievery—
None of her own doing.
How can evil be undone
And wounds be uninflicted
When time cannot be reversed?
Justice knows its hour.
The meek shall reign,
The last are first, the first are last,
Those who tower are razed.
If not within the time me we know,
Then far beyond our knowledge.
When a thousand years are as a day
When all is well with humble souls,
And earthly wrongs are righted.

SHADOWS

Take my hand.
Descend with me
To a secret place
That light never reaches.
Only a shadowy presence there,
Nothing to be feared.
It only begs to see the light,
Something it shouldn't do.
Set free, it will run amok,
And all who witness will wonder,
What kind of caretakers are we?
Its freedom can only be
Deep in the bowels of darkness.
Worm with me through twists and turns,
Our footpaths slimed and muddy,
Walls press in, and ceilings plunge,
Until we crawl on our bellies,
Wallowing in fetid muck,
Mingling with rats and leeches,
Like snakes and slugs, slithering.
In total darkness, with
Only sounds to guide us,
A mournful moan finds our ears
And draws us ever deeper.
Be strong I urge,
We must resist.
But, how? you ask—

Hear his pitiful wails?
No, I growl. Listen not.
Unless you fall for its appeals,
Slyly crafted to hypnotize,
And induce you to set it free.
Besides, it's not human.
Not human?
You've seen him?
No, I say with chagrin
I could never go that far.
Then why should I listen to you?
You don't even know
If he's a him or a her.
Rising to argue with greater force,
My crown bangs a rock.
Jaw shudders from the jolt,
Molar slams molar,
Tongue sandwiched between.
I wince.
We've gone too far, I cry.
Crabbing backward for a bit
Is our only way of retreat.
You poke my rump.
Keep going, you prod.
I reply emphatically, NO,
We're farther than I ever go.
You shove me again,
Demanding to know
How I can tell what's ahead
When I've never been there before.
We're not going back, you insist.
Stuck here I am

Between you and new
No room to advance,
You refuse to retreat,
And somehow, it knows
The jam I'm in,
Its pleading grows ever louder
The longer I'm trapped where I am.
I have to admit
Once, I held the idea
When I first heard its
Groaning below,
Whoever it was,
Whatever its plight,
Maybe, we could be friends.
Everyone said I was dumb,
I should never believe
Humans live underfoot—
A stupid notion, I know.
But try as I might
The idea never died.
It haunts me even today.
Fine. We'll go.
For a few feet more
The passage grows tighter,
Testing my resolve.
Then an aura, subdued,
Like a lure to a perch,
Takes my reason in tow,
Drawing me into
A cavernous space
Where echoes careen
Off limestone walls,

And *it* sits caged before us.
It.
It moans.
It cajoles.
It pleads.
It taunts.
It screams.
I yell back,
Shut up!
But while I glare,
You approach the thing
And simply inquire,
What do you need?
It answers, politely at that,
Please, I would like some light.
Offering it your hand,
Come, you say,
Then together we three ascend,
And I learn my fears were mere folly.

ELEMENTS

WIND

Wind shrills through barren branches
Draws groans from forest depths
Rustles fallen leaves
Ripples over steel-blue waters
Laps foamy crests of waves
Whistles though runners' teeth
Wisps the napes of wary necks,
Sends shivers down the spine,
Stings desiccated skin and eyes,
Its icy blades unsheathed
Cuts deep to the bone,
Pummels rocky canyon walls
Provoking dreadful moans,
Blasts boulders, crags, and hoodoos
Reducing them to dust,
Leaves men cowering in its face and
Trees bowing in its wake,
Powers sloops across the seas,
Feeds the buzz of life on shore.

RAIN

Minuscule prisms
Reflecting morning light
Ballet in gentle breezes,
Elevating the soul.
Gray skies subdue nature's colors,
Giving rest to weary eyes.
Curtains of dense, watery beads
Cool the skin,
Refresh the spirit,
Add miles to an afternoon walk.
Vapors rising from musty logs
Or newly cut grass
Infuse an earthy flavor
Into each new breath.
Gritty urban streets
Washed by heavenly sprinklers
Restore humanity,
At least for a while.
Torrents spilling from clouds
Fill lakes and ponds,
Springs and streams,
Estuaries and oceans
With a fundamental need.
There is no better way
To dance or sing or play
Than in the rain.

FIRE

Lanterns mark midnight paths,
Hearthstones vanquish winter chills,
Infernos purge blighted forests,
Liquid iron refines as steel,
Rods bend in blacksmiths' forges,
A Phoenix from ashen remnants rises,
Hope and courage in crucibles meld.
When harnessed by well-intended hands
Fire transmutes able into is,
But gripped by greedy talons,
Fire devours the best of souls.

STARS

Pricked into sapphire skies,
Igniting hope and awe,
Stars etch legends in timeless space,
Point the way on open seas,
Reveal predestined courses,
Veil God from mortal eyes,
Tug us homeward bound,
Gracefully, as we age into eternal realms.

ESSAYS

INDIGO

Let's get something straight right off the top. Indigo isn't a color—and if you have to ask the question that's nibbling at your mind, you'll never understand.

Indigo isn't a snowflake—white. White is blind to color, erasing perceptions of depth, shades and outlines that define individuality, causing us to stumble over obstacles feet cannot read. Neither is it sympathy, understanding, nor any other voluntary act. Indigo is the unconscious absorption of another's colors—crying their tears, shrieking their cries, bearing their terror, anguish, emptiness, despair, loneliness, horror, trepidation, hopelessness, helplessness, all forms of darkness as if each emotion were our own.

It's the choke in a throat, the pinch in a heart, which springs from another's wounds.

It's finding ourselves embedded under the thin skin of someone who can't 'just get over it.'

It's drowning in waves of helplessness when good people do bad things out of willfulness or ignorance or both.

It's feeling things too deeply when there's no way over to the shallow end.

Indigo is the terror in a child's eyes who's denied a mother's embrace by black holes called abduction, abandonment, neglect, war, death, or known by any other name. There's no point labeling the color of her pupils—some hue of brown, blue, or green? The scratchy whites of her delicate eyes are webbed in red.

It's the tortured memory of a parent's lips once probed by a child's fingers, joy forever lost in the abyss of unjust law and order.

It's the binding pang of a stomach filled with emptiness and roiling with despair.

It's hopelessness when the lust for power trumps the inalienable rights of the 'least of these'.

It's anger over the dehumanization of those who are different.

It's the waning essence—the aspirating self—leaching out as passersby see only the concrete into which margins are absorbed.

It's the void that opens in one's soul as the gaping throat of war gulps down each parent, widow, orphan child, brother, sister, closest friend whose warrior comes home maimed, dead, or not at all. We never heal from these wounds; we only cauterize the flow of grief. The best we can hope is that seventy or a hundred-and-fifty years from now, the cancer that invaded our body politic will not return and make us fight again for that which should never be open to debate.

Indigo measures trauma on a scale color can't comprehend, because wounds defy conventions like magnitude or degree. The aftermath of each transgression is rubble—brick and capstone alike pounded into dust. Indigo is a condition no one chooses, it takes us. It's the bittersweet grace of god clawing at our hearts as we grapple with the insanity of man feeding off fellow man.

HEALING

Blackened spikes protrude from smoldering hillsides, a landscape formerly dressed in piney greens, burnt siennas, and stalwart browns that stood against an azure sky. Tangled Manzanita, which once blanketed a nearby slope, resembles twisted rebar scattered over an abandoned junkyard. All that's left of my cabin—save a blistered metal roof—are soot-smudged stones, bluish-grey steel beams, and chaotic heaps of charred timbers.

I lamented that sight years ago in the wake of an inferno that decimated memories and dashed hopes of a waltz with nature. My heart was empty then of all but grief, longing, confusion, fear, despair, bitterness, betrayal. Since that day, rains have fallen, melding ash with earth and seed. Moons have risen, promising rest. Dawns illumined new beginnings. The sun gave warmth. Buds sprouted. Blossoms unfolded. Fruit broadcast its seeds over regenerated soil.

If I could pick one moment to exist, if I am allotted one speck of time to linger, to be, to escape the calamities of life, shall I dance forever in the rain, rest under the everlasting moon, live only for the dawn, bask under a perpetual sun, hold petals tightly in unfurled buds, or hang forever pregnant above the fertile loam?

Perhaps I will persist through relentless floods, sunless winters, and cloudless droughts to become tinder for another avarice firestorm, and left gazing blurry-eyed upon my life's devastation—empty of all but grief, longing, confusion, fear, despair, bitterness, and betrayal, crying, "Vanity. Vanity. Everything is vanity."

Or can I heal ... find wholeness ... invest fully in each speck of time ... embrace every moment as if it is all the time there is, as if it is my only moment of grace ... growing wiser and stronger than before.

TYRONE

All was quiet that moonlit night when the alarm sounded. A boy had fled into the woods, carrying a kitchen knife and threatening to kill anyone who tried to bring him back. He was Tyrone—over six-feet, sweet sixteen, lean, athletic build, never caused trouble before. Rare for kids from Watts, in 1968.

Someone said he had seizures, got embarrassed and feared he'd be teased if his body started shaking, if he thrashed on the ground, frothing at the mouth, biting his tongue until the foam turned pink. Only a few joined the search, beating through brush and thickets, calling his name, wary of the knife.

Time stands still when we're desperate. It also rushes past, adding confusion to chaos. Someone finally shouted, he's down by the lake!

When I reached the water's edge, he raised the knife over his head and demanded that we retreat, leave him alone. Or else he'd resort to violence on himself or anyone who approached. I don't understand why, but I did the opposite. My hands outstretched, I waded in. His eyes darted back and forth, checking those gawking along the shore, tracking my knees as they disappeared below the lake's shimmering sheath. When my hips began to sink as well, he locked his gaze on mine. I took that as a cue.

In a steady voice, I pledged to keep him safe, shield him from teasing. He could sleep in my tent. I'd stand guard outside. I stopped an arm's length away. Ripples lapped at my waist as I offered him my hand.

He stared at my open, upturned palm. Tears trickled down his cheek, his mouth paralyzed in confusion. Then his eyes met mine again, and he handed me the knife. After a long embrace—like him clutching a life ring, tossed from a passing ship—we waded in to shore, my arm draped over his neck.

At dawn, we loaded into a rickety old bus, and wound down the mountain to LA. Kids and counselors glanced back at us every now and then. The driver stole peeks in his rearview mirror. What I mainly recall about Tyrone today, is his hand holding my ankle as he slept on the floor of the bus all the way back to Watts.

In the Fall of that year, a student crawled up on the red brick steps of the house where he lived. He bled out in the cool night air—they said a victim of a young black man wielding a long-blade knife across the street from a fraternity house.

Only days before, two blocks away, in the lobby of the house where I lived, I sat down on a piano bench next to a stranger whose hands floated over the keyboard, lightly touching ivories, black and white, as I watched in awe and drank in his soulful voice. That's all I recall of the color of his skin. Several days later, police arrested him, for a murder on fraternity row.

Looking back after all these years I can't help but wonder how Tyrone turned out. Did he meet the same fate as that musical stranger? Did he continue to be the same scared, sweet soul who stood in that lake handing over that knife? Did he die in a rice paddy in Vietnam when he turned eighteen, fighting someone else's war? Whatever the case, I'll always miss Tyrone.

EARTH

A child stands before her father who sits ensconced in his favorite chair, perusing the evening paper. On the front page a photo—the image of earth taken from a satellite—grips the girl's attention. A younger brother soon appears at her side and, surrendering to impatience, he begins to nag.

The father, unable to ignore his children's presence, peers over the newsprint barricade and notices the gravitational pull of the photograph on his daughter's imagination. He tears the picture from the newspaper, dissects it into manageable pieces, and presents it to the young intruders. He instructs them not to come back until they have reassembled the world. When the children return in a short time, he reminds them they must complete their assignment unassisted. In unison, they reply, "We did."

Perplexed, the father examines their work and exclaims, "How did you do it so fast?"

The girl responds, naïve to the world's complexity, "On the back of the world were the faces of children. When the children were right the world was, too."

A world of right children, how difficult could that be?

Children sift freshly turned soil through curious fingers, their faces screwed up in wonder.

Children dance in summer showers, tongues licking dewy air, and in winter they feast on icy flakes of snow.

Children run barefoot over carpets of sod, inhaling the scent of newly mowed grass.

Children toss leaves in autumn's brisk gusts, raining down color, varied and vibrant, implanting memories of earth's rich taste.

Bathing in the sun's embrace, children fuse with earth as if folding into their mother's breasts.

Children embrace life as one timeless whole, rejoicing at its mere existence and grieving the loss of its tiniest part.

Children offer their faces, unabashed, to the kisses of dogs and cats and orca whales. They smooth the coats of lambs and fawns and squeal at the touch of scaly fish, stare in wonder at long-necked giraffes, marvel at the sight of elephants' trunks, giggle at a pig's grunts and snouts, curl in bed with their favorite pets. Then there's their love affair with a newborn calf or foal, or cuddle time with baby chicks. Most precious of all is their unbridled tears over losing one of these.

It isn't we who make the world right; it's the world that calls us gently to its bosom. But, deaf to Mother Earth we wander from her voice and wonder—where do all the children go?

www.ingramcontent.com/pod-product-compliance
Lightning Source LLC
Chambersburg PA
CBHW030812090426
42736CB00028B/1334